Dedication Page

I dedicate this book to my Dada (Grandma), who taught me the beauty of Ramadan and helped me write this story. Thank you for sharing your wisdom and love with me."

"To my little brother, Zaim—may we always celebrate Ramadan together, learning and growing side by side." Ramadan Mubarak!

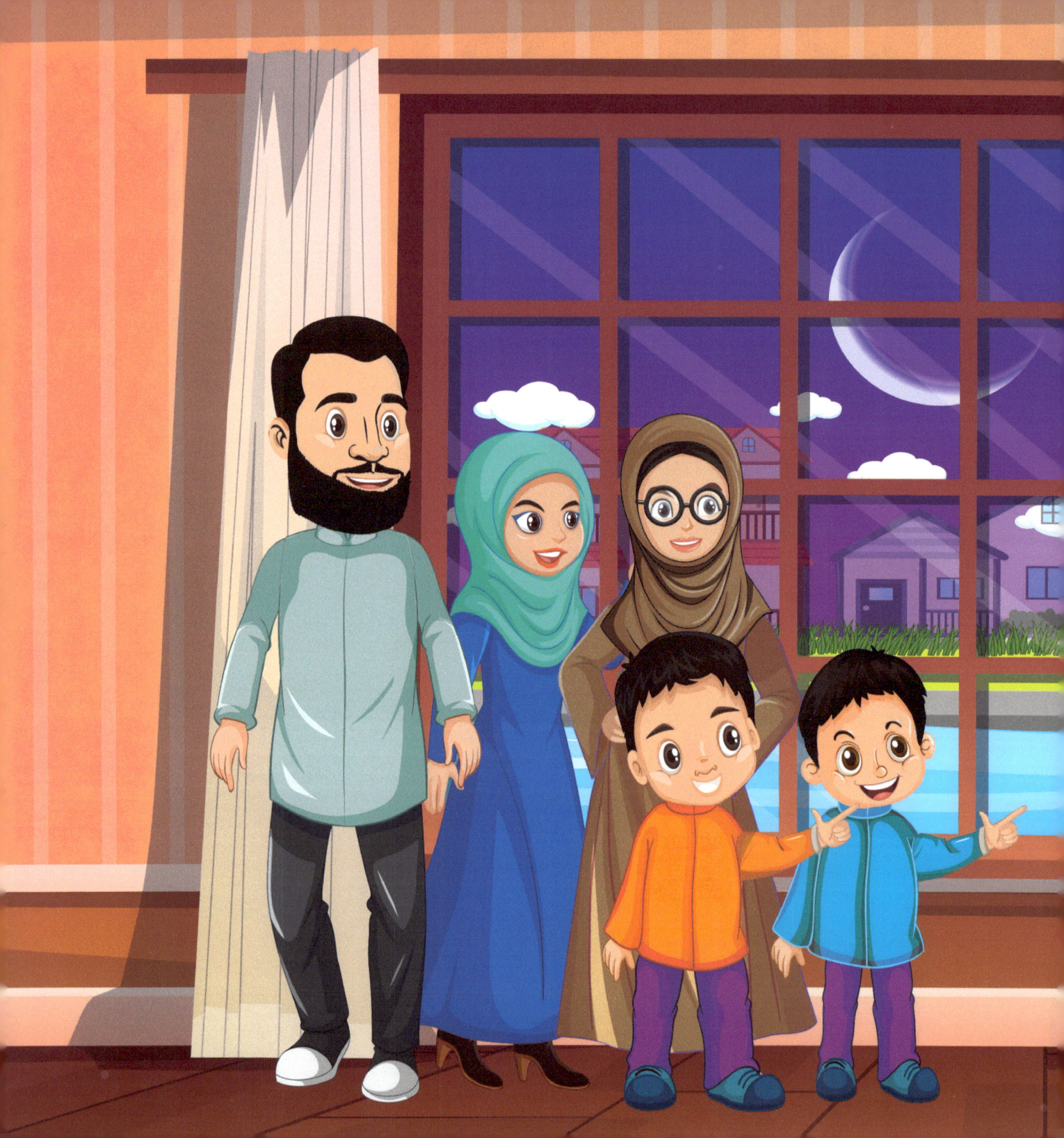

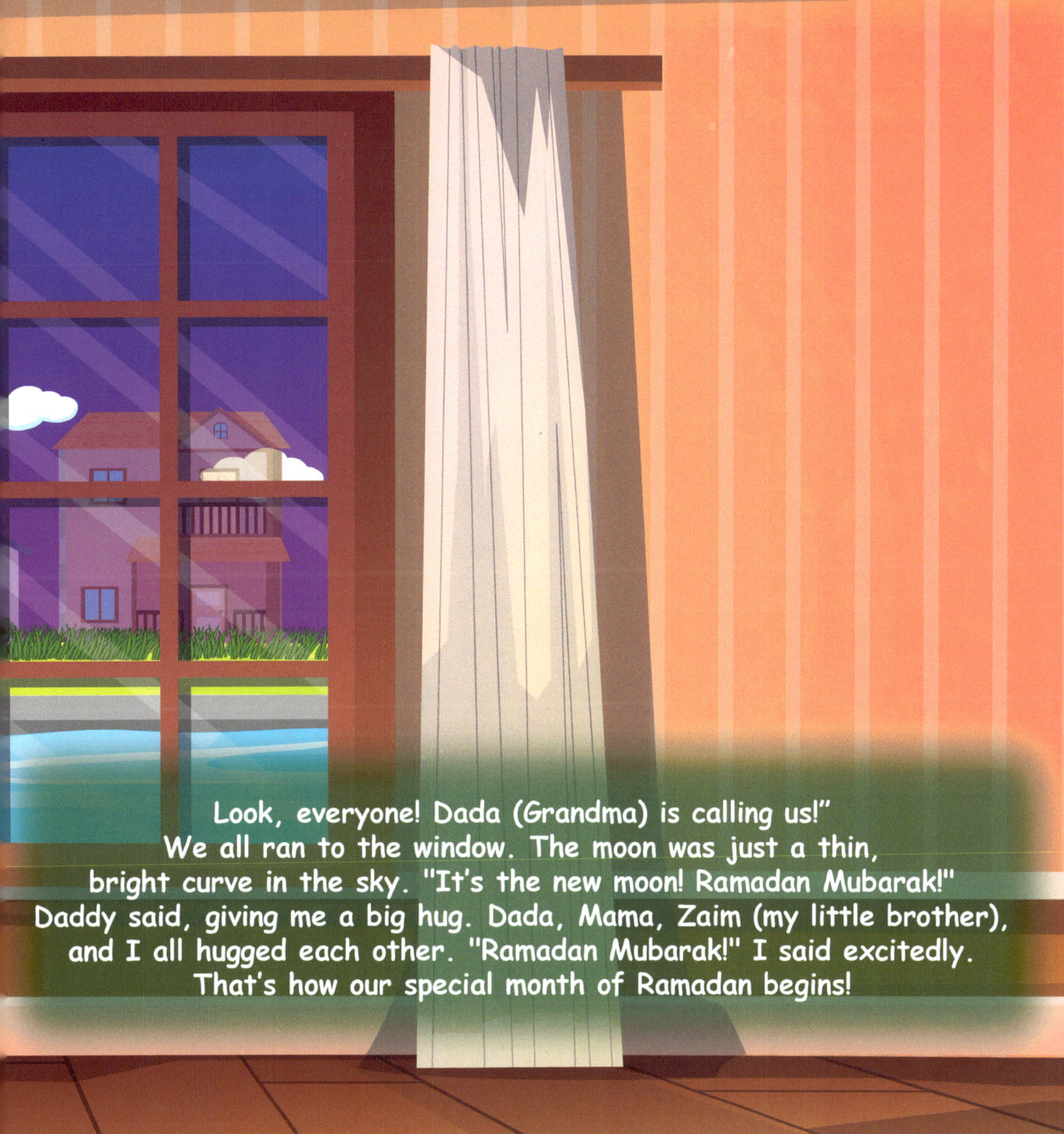

Look, everyone! Dada (Grandma) is calling us!"
We all ran to the window. The moon was just a thin,
bright curve in the sky. "It's the new moon! Ramadan Mubarak!"
Daddy said, giving me a big hug. Dada, Mama, Zaim (my little brother),
and I all hugged each other. "Ramadan Mubarak!" I said excitedly.
That's how our special month of Ramadan begins!

After hugs, Dada called us to sit with her.
"Come, Sareem & Zaim, let's learn about Ramadan!"
she said.
She opened the Quran and read a beautiful
verse about Ramadan:
"The month of Ramadan is the one in which the Quran was sent
down as guidance for mankind…" (Surah Al-Baqarah 2:185)
Then, Dada closed the Quran and told us a story from the Hadith.
"Over 1,400 years ago, our beloved Prophet Muhammad (peace be upon him)
would go to a quiet cave called Hira to think and pray.
One night, something amazing happened!"
Zaim and I leaned in closer.

"Angel Jibreel (Gabriel) came to him and said, 'Iqra!'"
"What does that mean?" I asked.
It means 'Read!'" Dada smiled. "That was the first word revealed to our
Prophet (Peace Be Upon Him).He was scared at first, but his wife,
Khadijah (may Allah be pleased with her), comforted him.
Soon, more verses of the Quran were revealed, guiding us
to live as good Muslims."
Mama added, "That's why Ramadan is so special—it's the month
when the Quran began to be revealed."
Daddy nodded. "And fasting teaches us patience, kindness,
and gratitude. When we don't eat all day, we understand how poor
people feel, so we help by giving food, clothes,
and money to those in need.

Sareem, wake up!" Dada whispered early in the morning.
Before I even opened my eyes, I smelled something delicious.
I ran to the kitchen. Mama had made a big breakfast.
The table was full of yummy food! We sat together and ate
Suhoor. After eating, Daddy led us in Fajr prayer, our morning prayer.
"Did you know we pray five times a day?" Daddy said.

he Islamic calendar.
during Ramadan.
unset.
ience, and gratitude.
in need.

At school, my teacher smiled and said, "Ramadan Mubarak, Sareem!"
I was surprised. "How do you know about Ramadan, Ms. Teacher?"
She smiled. "Would you like to share about Ramadan with
your classmates?"
I felt a little shy, but I nodded. She let me sit in her chair at
the morning meeting.
"Good morning, everyone! Today, I'll tell you about Ramadan!"

the Islamic calendar.
during Ramadan.
sunset.
atience, and gratitude.
in need

I took a deep breath and began.
"Ramadan is our holy month. Muslims around the world fast
from sunrise to sunset." I told them how
Prophet Muhammad (peace be upon him) broke his fast
with dates and water 1,400 years ago.
"We still follow this today! After sunset, we eat Iftar, our big meal."
"Ramadan teaches us patience, kindness, and giving charity."
My dad had donated some Ramadan books to the school,
so my teacher read one after my talk.
I felt proud!

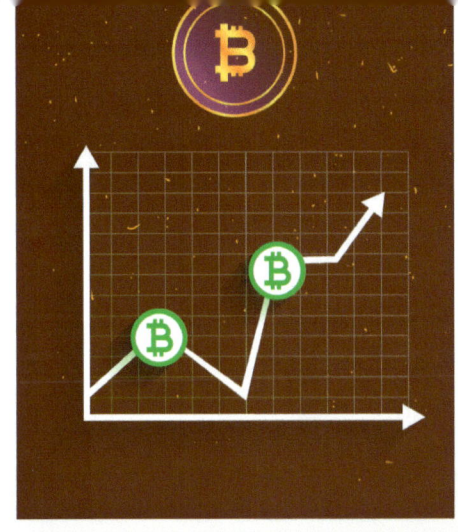

When I got home, Mama said, "Take a rest, Sareem. We are going to the masjid later to break our fast." Dada came to my room.
"As-salamu alaykum, Sareem," she greeted me.
"Wa alaykum as-salam, Dada!" I replied.
"Do you know what that means?" she asked.
"Yes! It means 'May Allah's peace be with you!'"
Dada smiled. "And when you say 'Wa alaykum as-salam,' you're saying 'And upon you be peace!'"

Before I knew it, Daddy was waking me up.
"Sareem, wake up! It's time to go to the masjid for Iftar!"
We all got dressed and headed to Worcester Islamic Center.
The masjid was full of people! There were at least 500 people there!
Daddy, Zaim, and I sat upstairs with the men, while Mama
and Dada went to the women's section.

As soon as the Adhan (call to prayer) was heard, we all said "Bismillah" and took a sip of water. I ate a date just like Prophet Muhammad (Peace be upon him) did!
Everyone was smiling, eating together, and sharing food.
After eating, the kids played while the adults continued eating and talking. "Mama is helping serve food!" Dada said, pointing to the women's section.
I felt happy seeing her helping others.

After Iftar, we heard the Adhan for Isha, calling everyone to prayer. The masjid was filled with silence as everyone prepared for Salah. Soon, the Iqamah was called—the second call signaling that prayer was about to begin. Everyone lined up behind the Imam, standing shoulder to shoulder.

After Isha, we prayed Taraweeh, a special Ramadan prayer only performed in this month. Each night, the Imam recites different parts of the Quran, and by the end of Ramadan, many masjids finish the entire Quran! "The masjid was full, and I felt peaceful praying with so many people. When we got home, I could barely keep my eyes open. "Thank you, Allah, for this beautiful day of Ramadan," I whispered as I snuggled into bed.
Before I knew it, my eyes were closing

FOOD TRUCK

At the end of Ramadan, we celebrate Eid al-Fitr!
We wear new clothes and go to the masjid for the Eid prayer.
Thousands of Muslims gather to pray and say, "Eid Mubarak!"
After prayer, we visit family and friends, eat delicious food,
and share gifts. My favorite part? At one auntie's house,
there's always an ice cream truck waiting for us!

That's how we celebrate Ramadan and Eid!

"Eid Mubarak, everyone!" I said with a big smile.
Ramadan teaches us kindness, patience, and gratitude.
And I can't wait for next year!

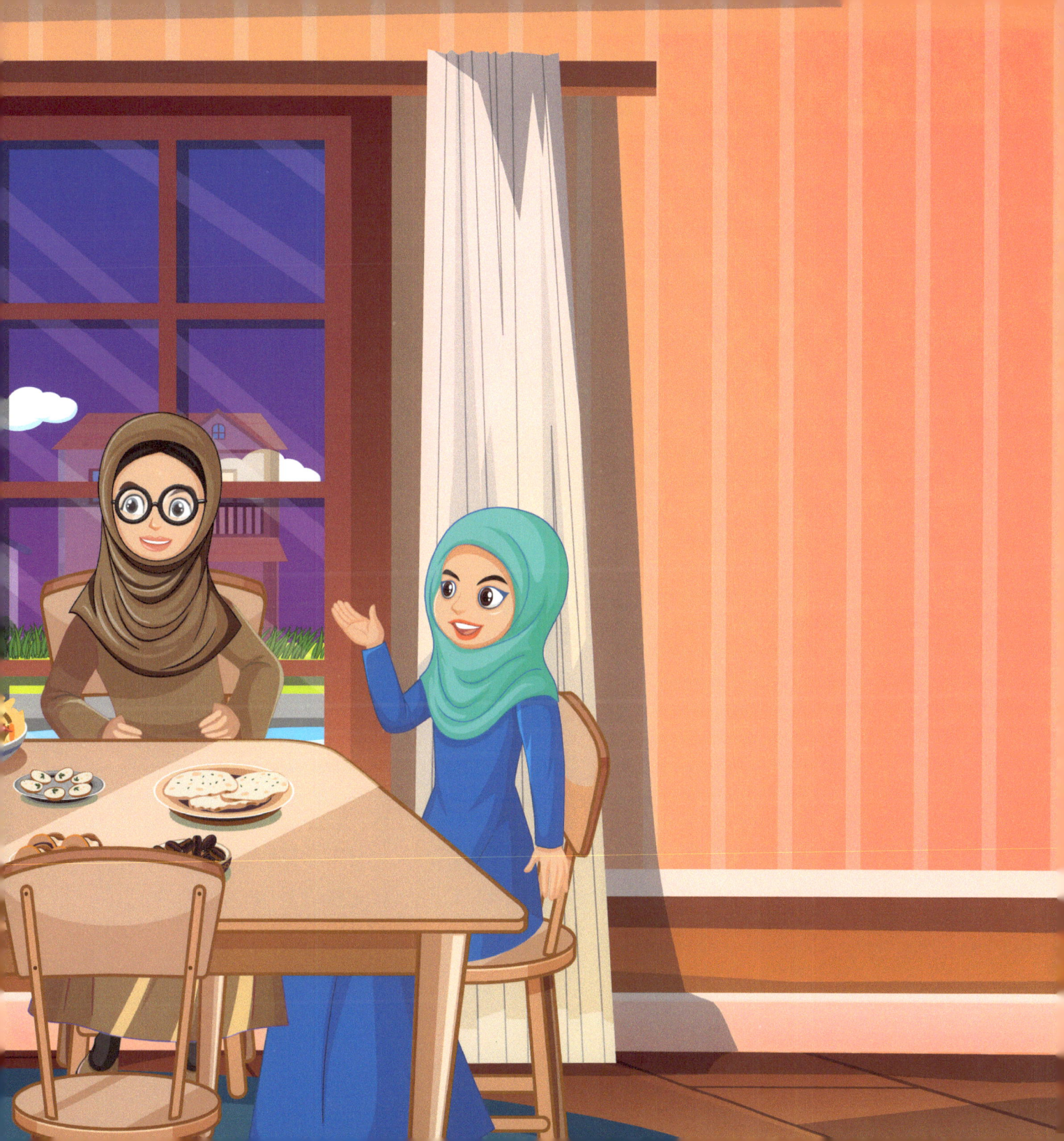

Author

Sareem is a young storyteller who loves sharing his adventures! After writing his first book, Sareem's Lemonade Stand, he is excited to share Sareem's Ramadan to help kids learn about this special month. He hopes his books inspire children to explore, learn, and have fun!

Co-Author

Sabina Chowdhury is Sareem's grandmother and the co-author of this book. With over 30 years of experience as a writer and poet in her native language, Bengali, she has always been passionate about storytelling. She created this book with Sareem to help children understand the beauty of Ramadan and its values of faith, kindness, and gratitude. Sabina is proud of her grandsons, Sareem and Zaim, and hopes this book inspires young readers everywhere.

www.ingramcontent.com/pod-product-compliance
Lightning Source LLC
Chambersburg PA
CBHW041612120626

46551CB00002B/409